Oh, Josephine!

Tess Franklin
Illustrated by Jackie Moss

CELEBRATION PRESS
Pearson Learning Group

Josephine is my big sister who now lives in an apartment of her own. Josephine is very smart and EXCEPTIONALLY NEAT.

Mom can't think who she gets it from—like the measles—or how Josephine came to be her child. Josephine's hair is dark and her eyes are blue, and she's EXCEPTIONALLY NEAT.

I'm like Mom. Our hair is mousy brown and our eyes are mousy gray and we are not neat at all.

In our house, sometimes the cat sleeps on top of the refrigerator, and sometimes the dog sleeps in the bathtub. I sleep in every bed in the house—one by one. When all of them are messy, I start in the first again; and when the mood takes her, Mom smoothes the sheets, and shakes the blankets and the pillows. This suits Mom and me very well.

Mom made the mistake of telling Josephine that we are off on a vacation to the Emerald Coast to visit Mom's brother, Hamish. My Uncle Hamish and Mom have a lot in common because sometimes he sleeps in the bathtub and sometimes the dog sleeps in his bed and his cat sleeps in the drawer with his mismatched socks.

The day before we are to leave, Josephine is home for lunch. She comes on Sundays, and after we've eaten the great food Mom cooks, Josephine insists that we wash the dishes—and the pots too—right away! Then she makes coffee in the coffee pot! Mom uses anything . . . a jug, a vase, or the teapot. It suits Mom and me this way very well.

"Oh, Josephine," Mom lets out a moan when Josephine says brightly: "I'll housesit while you're away."

It's lucky Mom doesn't have to think up a reason to say "No," because our friend Mitzi is going to feed the animals and "keep an eye on things."

"Mitzi!" Josephine frowns, knowing Mitzi is kind but not EXCEPTIONALLY NEAT. "Oh well, if you're sure."

"I'm sure," Mom says as Josephine jumps up and takes the clock out of a tin stuffed with cotton balls because Mom doesn't like to hear the alarm ring.

"I'll just wash your car," Josephine says as she puts the clock on the mantel, where it doesn't belong, between the cough medicine and a box of mothballs. She tut-tuts. "You can't drive to the Emerald Coast in that dirtball."

"Oh, Josephine," Mom murmurs before my sister goes whistling off to the garage, which I suppose some people would see as a mess.

Soon she's back. "Where is the car wax?" she asks. "I want to do a good job."

"Oh, Josephine," Mom sighs, but we find the car wax with the bird seed and my slippers in the rabbit cage.

Now our car doesn't look like our car, and Josephine is saying, "I'll help you pack."

"Oh, Josephine," Mom's smile resembles a toothache because she's forgotten where the suitcases are.

Josephine insists on helping so we search and find one. It's full of cans of dog food as well as an electric heater, which needs fixing; and Christmas decorations; and the red, white, and blue yarn Mom intended knitting into a sweater for Josephine when she was still at school; and pressed flowers; and photos; and 10 soup spoons; and parts of a spinning wheel.

The other suitcase turns up in the trunk of our now-cleaned-and-waxed car, but where is the key?

"Clothes," says Josephine, still bright. "Your clothes to pack."

Mom's face is pale, and she gets twitchy around her mouth.

"Oh, Josephine," Mom tries to rally a smile. "You've done enough."

"No trouble," says Josephine, leaping from room to room as if on a treasure hunt. Sandals, socks, jeans, T-shirts, jackets, hats . . . she works up from our feet to our heads in what, we guess, is an EXCEPTIONALLY NEAT way. The Moon is high and the stars are out by the time Josephine collects everything she wants us to take.

"Oh, Josephine," Mom pleads, but Josephine washes and irons everything before she packs. Then she pushes the cat off the refrigerator and the dog out of the bath. After Josephine kisses Mom and me on both cheeks in an EXCEPTIONALLY NEAT way, she's off, but not before she cheerfully reminds us that Mitzi can be forgetful so she had better have a key to the house . . . just in case.

"Oh, Josephine." With a grudging grin, Mom unwillingly hands over our spare key, which I remembered was in a peanut butter jar in the bread box. Josephine pops the key into her bag, which is square and EXCEPTIONALLY NEAT.

The next day Mom hurls wet suits and swimsuits and snorkels and in-line skates and boogie boards and books and every spare this and that into the car.

"What a relief," squeals Mom, as she finds one of the hens has laid an egg on the front seat and the dog is gnawing a bone in the back.

At last we drive north, and we're well along the coast before we even try to remember if we closed the windows and locked the door. When we reach Uncle Hamish's house, we find it's a home away from home.

One sunny morning as we eat ginger pudding for
breakfast, with Uncle Hamish's parrot sitting on his
shoulder and one of his white mice sitting on mine,
the telephone rings.

"I'll answer it," says Mom. Her face is troubled when she comes back.

"That was Mitzi telephoning from New York."

"New York!"

"Yes. Family matters."

Uncle Hamish crumbles toast for a lizard as Mom's face looks more troubled, like a real storm brewing.

"It could be a bad dream." She bites her lip. "A nightmare. We should leave for home. Now!"

"Why?"

Mom's eyes bulge. "Because Mitzi asked Josephine to housesit OUR HOUSE when she left."

"Oh, Josephine." Uncle Hamish hunches his shoulders
and frowns. Worried, he looks over the top of his glasses
and pictures Josephine . . . very smart but
EXCEPTIONALLY NEAT, too. Then, halfway to calm, he
remembers Josephine's visit to the Emerald Coast.
"It took me a year to recover," he tells Mom. "Hannah,
you must keep her away from here. Of course, I'm fond
of Josephine, but the way I live suits me very well."

Mom pats his hand, and Uncle Hamish cheers up. When he waves us off, he has wise parting words for Mom and consoling words for me: "Don't worry. You'll fix things . . . in time."

AND WE WILL, BECAUSE:

The dog is clipped, and his tail drags between his legs.

The cat smells of flea powder and hisses instead of purrs.

The rabbits are still only a pair.

AND:

Beds are made. Toothpaste, shampoo, and soap are in the bathroom.

The lawn mower and a sack of grass seed are in the garden shed.

Sheets and towels are in the linen closet.

Books are on the bookshelves and magazines, in the magazine rack.

The iron and the ironing board, as well as the clothes basket, are in the laundry.

The umbrellas are in the hall.

The pots and pans, the toaster, the juicer, and the mixer are all in the kitchen.

The plates are in the cupboards.

The knives, forks, and spoons are in the drawers.

The birdseed is in the bird cage.

The wood is in a basket by the fireplace.

AND THERE'S MORE:

She had watered the plants, scoured the stove, washed our curtains, tied up the old newspapers Mom kept to read "one day," cleaned the windows, taken our shoes to the shoemaker, and weeded the garden.

"Oh, Josephine," Mom wails as she opens cupboards to peep in.

Everything that needs a lid has a lid AND THEY FIT. Everything has a label marked in EXCEPTIONALLY NEAT and easy-to-read writing.

AS FOR MY ROOM ...

"Oh, Josephine." Mom flops down on a sofa without having to push anything off, then her head sinks to her hands as if she's visiting a gloomy place she doesn't often go to.

However, it's not long before she sits up, notices her favorite blanket neatly folded on a table and tosses it over the sofa arm. Next she scatters magazines about and one lands on the floor.

By the following Sunday:

Mom started out to dye her hair red, and it turned out green.

The dog has chewed the front doormat and started on the back one.

Our vacation pictures are glued to our mirror in the hall.

The fish tank has stopped bubbling, and the fish are happy in a tin tub we found under the house for a rainy day.

"Oh, Mother!" Josephine cries when she arrives for Sunday lunch. Things are back to normal for Mom and me, and that suits us very well.